P9-ECV-879

a gift for

_____

from

Inspired by the 1950s landmark photographic exhibition, *"The Family of Man,"* M.I.L.K. began as an epic global search to develop a collection of extraordinary and geographically diverse images portraying humanity's Moments of Intimacy, Laughter and Kinship (M.I.L.K.). This search took the form of a photographic competition – probably the biggest, and almost certainly the most ambitious of its kind ever to be conducted. With a world-record prize pool, and renowned Magnum photographer Elliott Erwitt as Chief Judge, the M.I.L.K. competition attracted 17,000 photographers from 164 countries. Three hundred winning images were chosen from the over 40,000 photographs submitted to form the basis of the M.I.L.K. Collection.

The winning photographs were first published as three books titled *Family, Friendship* and *Love* in early 2001, and are now featured in a range of products worldwide, in nine languages in more than 20 countries. The M.I.L.K. Collection also forms the basis of an international travelling exhibition.

The M.I.L.K. Collection portrays unforgettable images of human life, from its first fragile moments to its last. They tell us that the rich bond that exists between families and friends is universal. Representing many diverse cultures, the compelling and powerful photographs convey feelings experienced by people around the globe. Transcending borders, the M.I.L.K. imagery reaches across continents to celebrate and reveal the heart of humanity.

www.milkphotos.com

FAMILIES

with love

MOMENTS INTIMACY LAUGHTER KINSHIP

Other things may change us,
but we start and end with family.

[ANTHONY BRANDT]

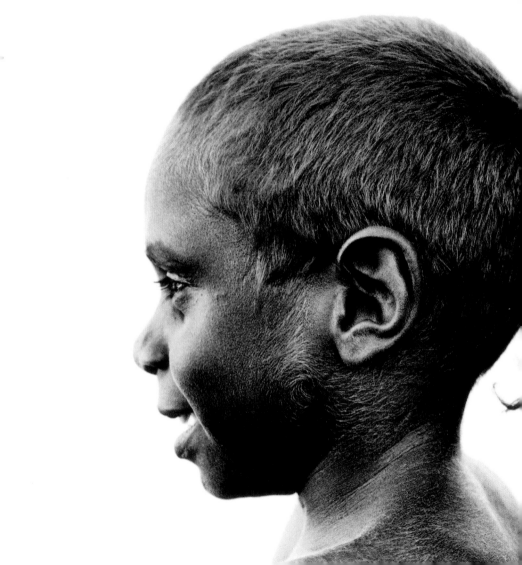

Without the human
community,
one single human being
cannot survive.

[DALAI LAMA]

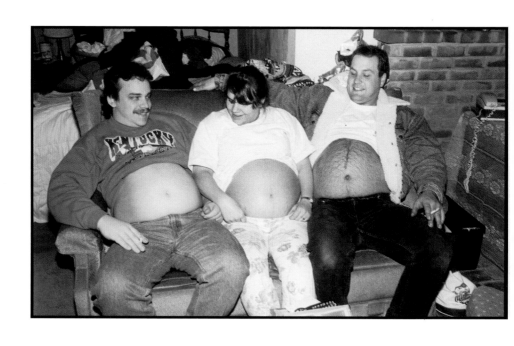

It is the **absurdity** of family life, the raggedness of it, . . .

that is at once its redemption and its true nobility.

[JAMES MCBRIDE]

Seek the **wisdom** of the ages, but look at the world through the eyes of a child.

[RON WILD]

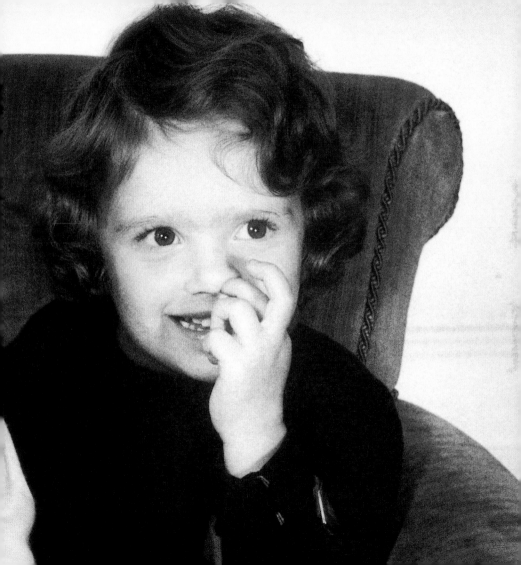

Children's faces looking up,
holding **wonder**
like a cup.

[SARA TEASDALE]

So sweet and precious is family life . . .

[JAMES MCBRIDE]

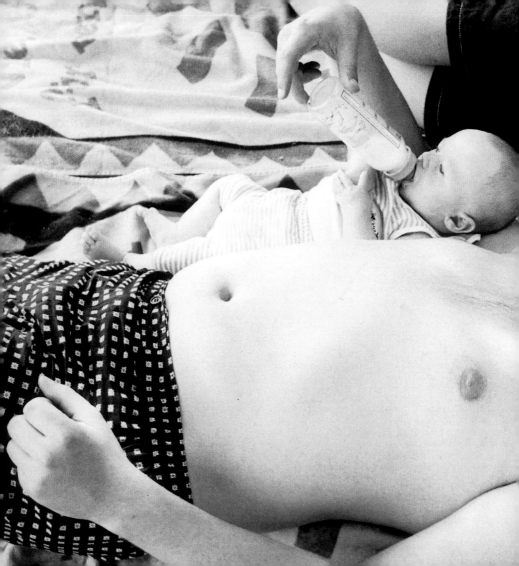

I live for those who love me,
for those who know me true.

[GEORGE LINNAEUS BANKS]

Family faces are magic mirrors.

[GAIL LUMET BUCKLEY]

Having a place to go —
is a home.

Having someone to love —
is a family.

[DONNA HEDGES]

The family – that dear octopus
from whose tentacles we never quite escape,
nor in our innermost hearts
quite wish to.

[DOROTHY GLADYS SMITH]

The family is one of nature's masterpieces.

[GEORGE SANTAYANA]

Family is the last and greatest
discovery . . . It is our last miracle.

[JAMES MCBRIDE]

Pages 32–33

© Sayyed Nayyer Reza, Pakistan
Love and kindness bridge the generation gap in Lahore, Pakistan. Nine-year-old Suman shares a playful moment with her elderly friend and neighbor – the old lady is known simply as Amman, an Urdu word for "mother."

Pages 34–35 and back cover

© Mikhail Evstafiev, Russia
On the streets of Santiago de Cuba, Cuba – a couple's uninhibited display of affection raises a spontaneous smile from their young audience.

Page 37

© Lyn Dowling, Australia
"Ma" and me – Rebecca, aged 20 months, and her grandmother "Ma" share the simple pleasures of a street festival in Brisbane, Australia.

Page 38

© Ray Peek, Australia
Another generation learns about mustering from the head of the family. "Big" Morrie Dingle, a grazier in South Queensland, Australia, and his two grandsons take a break from the saddle to enjoy some food.

Page 39

© Roberto Colacioppo, Italy
A great-grandmother's heartfelt embrace of a young bride. The old lady, 97, and her great-granddaughter are the only family members who still live in the mountain village of Roccaspinalveti, Italy.

Pages 40–41

© Christopher Smith, USA
Age is no barrier to enjoying a dance at a wedding party in North Carolina, USA. New bride Pamela teaches Uncle Mac the steps, while the bride's parents show how it should be done.

Page 42

© Christel Dhuit, New Zealand
They may be twins, but their reactions are very different. Five-month-old sisters in Auckland, New Zealand.

Page 43

© Philip Kuruvita, Australia
A woodshed in Tasmania, Australia, provides an unusual playground for identical twins, Summer and Melody.

Page 45

© Jerry Koontz, USA
Liaza, aged 12, and her younger sister Adriana, six, at play on the streets of Ajijic village in Mexico.

Page 46

© Lambro (Tsiliyiannis), South Africa
Two-year-old Robert greets his 85-year-old grandfather, Christy, in Cape Town, South Africa.

Page 47

© Paul Carter, USA
A gentle smile from mother to son in Eugene, Oregon, USA. Nano, 85, suffers from arthritis but is cared for at home by her son, Doug. After an afternoon reading to his mother, Doug lifts her carefully back to bed.

Page 49

© Luca Trovato, USA
The Gobi Desert, Mongolia – stranded with all their belongings, a nomadic family are relaxed as they await help.

Pages 50–51

© Chirasak Tolertmongkol, Thailand
The sun sets over a hill tribe village in Chiang Rai, northern Thailand. While the parents gather in the middle of the village, their children use the main thoroughfare as their playground.

Pages 52–53

© Herman Krieger, USA
Surrounded by pictures of her loved ones, 92-year-old Frances reminisces on family life at her home in Oregon, USA.

Page 55

© Heather Pillar, Taiwan
Rob Schwartz with his father, Morrie. Mitch Albom, a writer and former student of Morrie, noticed Morrie on a television show and renewed contact with his old professor. The outcome was Albom's moving bestseller *Tuesdays with Morrie*, based on time spent with Morrie on the last 14 Tuesdays of his life.

Pages 56–57

© Andrei Jewell, New Zealand
The beautiful mountain scenery of Zanskar in the Indian Himalayas is the setting for a twilight stroll. In a region which is snow-covered for most of the year, Norbu and his young granddaughter make the most of the warm sunshine.

Page 59

© Thanh Long, Vietnam
In Phan Rang city, Vietnam, new life is nurtured by age-old experience as this 86-year-old grandmother shares a tender moment with her grandson.

What is a Helen Exley Giftbook?

Helen Exley Giftbooks cover the most powerful of all human relationships:
the bonds within families and between friends, and the theme of personal values.
No expense is spared in making sure that each book is as thoughtful and meaningful
a gift as it is possible to create: good to give, good to receive.
You have the results in your hands. If you have loved it – tell others!
There is no power on earth like the word-of-mouth recommendation of friends.

For a full list of Helen Exley's books, write to:
**Helen Exley Giftbooks at 16 Chalk Hill, Watford, WD19 4BG, UK,
or 185 Main Street, Spencer, MA 01562, USA, or visit
www.helenexleygiftbooks.com**

© 2004 PQ Publishers Limited. Published under license from M.I.L.K. Licensing Limited.

All copyrights of the photographic images are owned by the individual photographers
who have granted M.I.L.K. Licensing Limited the right to use them.

First published by Exley Publications Ltd in 2003, 16 Chalk Hill, Watford, Herts, WD19 4BG, UK.

4 6 8 10 12 11 9 7 5 3

ISBN 1 86187 605 X

A copy of the CIP data is available from the British Library on request. All rights reserved.
No part of this publication may be reproduced, stored in a retrieval system or transmitted
in any form by any means, electronic, mechanical, photocopying, recording or otherwise,
without the prior written permission of the publisher.

Concept designed by Kylie Nicholls. This edition designed by Holly Stevens. Printed in China.
Back cover quotation by George Santayana.

M · I · L · K ™
MOMENTS INTIMACY LAUGHTER KINSHIP